Subtitle: A little of my life

and a litt

MW00935837

Maybe I can change
someone's life or even
make them look at
their life as a blessing
and not a disaster.
Often, we get too
caught up in ourselves
and not stop to think
about others. Help
someone be great
today but do
understand everyone
can't come with you.

1

Printed in the United States of America

First Printing, 2017

ISBN-13:
978-1545318201

ISBN-10:
1545318204

Cover design by: Me

Photography by: Scott Weaver

Edits: Sheryl Hawes (Print) and Tehseen Fatima (Cover)

www.supportforeveryoung.com

Social Media -@Iamericayoung

TOC

Do me a fav & write down your struggle...

Dedication

I dedicate this book to strength and growth. It took me 4 long years to complete this book. Everything you read is from the heart. I give tough love so please do not take anything personal. Being that some of this was written in 2013, some things might have changed. I hope you all enjoy my very first book and may I inspire at least one person.

Introduction

I have been through it all. Being adopted really screwed my head up when I found out because I felt like I wasn't good enough. My mother had pretty much left me in the cold. The only question I have is WHY? In this book, I will talk about being left out as a child, my Mother & father as far as being adopted and not having them in my life. I will also talk about being a millionaire, my family, time, my first crush, people I have lost over the years, the street I grew up on, a thank you letter to my wonderful adopted mother, relationships, New York City and lastly some last words of one of my darkest secrets. Sit back and enjoy this ride. You should stay on your toes as you read this book. Thanks for the support!

Left Out

It's your first day of high school. When you got up this morning your focus was looking good and making sure the moment you stepped foot through those gates that you were noticed. That's a typical underclassman, right?

Most people probably thought I was the kid that didn't have to fit in. I got all my attention from my height and playing basketball. Little did they know, I wanted to hang with the pretty girls with the banging outfits, the nice shoes, and pounds of makeup. I am still learning, but it took me four years to realize that God had a plan for me that he had for no one else.

I wasn't the smartest apple on the tree and I hated school for the most part. Why did I fail every test I could possibly think of in high school? Why couldn't I be the first to raise my hand when the teacher asked a question? Why is it when I did raise my hand to answer a question I got it wrong and the other kids laughed at me? I would laugh with them just to try and make myself feel better, but the whole time they were laughing at me and not with me. Today I am here to let you know that if you're in this situation, I feel every bit of your pain.

The grass hasn't always been green for me. I never understood a lot of things that went on in my life, or why I had to go through the things I went through. My life wasn't horrible, but I have feelings and I want answers one day.

For one thing, I wish I had both parents. I wish I could have set down at the dinner table and fought over bread with my sisters and brothers. I wish I had the chance to go outside and play tag with them. But my life didn't turn out that way. I was some chick who grew up all alone in my auntie's house. Being the only child wasn't fun at all. I was dressed well and kept up, but I wanted the love from a mom and dad. That's what I was missing.

I am an attractive young woman, I have athleticism, and I'm smart enough to continue my education, but where was the love from my parents? My dad missed a lot of my life - keep reading to find out that situation.

The day I found out I was adopted, I felt like my life collapsed. That day my life changed completely. From then I knew I wanted to be better than my parents. I felt like a load was put on my shoulders and if I didn't make it to

the top then I would
regret it for the rest of
my life.

One hundred percent
of the time I have a smile
on my face or I'm laughing,
but little do others know
behind this smile is so
many questions and so
much confusion. As I get
older it gets harder
because I don't know how
to ask those tough
questions. I don't think I
have the guts to sit and
ask the questions. I don't
want the answers that
make my parents look
good. I want to know why
I was the kid left out, and
most importantly why
weren't my parents there
to love me? Life is too

short and I don't want to wait for the answers.

I'm pouring my heart out in this book and I just want you to sit back and see what it's like being Erica Young. I dedicate this chapter to every child that feels left out and has tons of questions.

Have you ever felt left out? Write it down and get it off your chest.

_____

_____

_____

.

She didn't want me?

Still to this day, I don't have a relationship with my biological mother. I never understood why she didn't raise me. I'm guessing because the streets were more important to her. Who wants to put their life on hold for 18 years to help someone else?

People tell me all the time I look like this stranger that birthed me. I'm not trying to sound mean and toss her in the dirt, but I want her to feel the pain that's been growing inside of me. I have spoken to her a couple of times on the phone and my main concern is I don't hear the pain in her voice of not being able to spend her life with me. That's the part that hurts the most.

Some of you have been adopted, raised by your aunts, grandmothers, etc., or maybe your mom passed away. No one understands. Outsiders think you're selfish and have a bad attitude. Yet they don't know the pain that's growing inside your heart. Has someone asked you are you okay and you hit them with a dry "yeah"?

Who can we turn to? Who understands our pain? Why didn't my mother raise me? Where is she and will she ever come back to get me? If you're going through something like this, then I want you to know that I understand your cry. I want you to go in your room and close the door, get on your knees, and just start praying to God. Scream, yell, holler, and let it all out. No matter what is going on in your life don't let people see you cry. It's a sign of fear and you don't want that. It took me a very long time to look at my story as a blessing and just accept it for what it is. When you're ready to give birth to your wonder unborn, make sure you love them unconditionally and do the things that you wish your mother could have done with you. Be better than her but love and respect her; she's still your mother.

I sit back and try to figure out all the reasons why my biological mother isn't here today and I can never seem to find an answer. God has everyone's life written out, and he knows exactly how your life will unfold before you do. So, God, you knew that my biological mother wasn't going to be here with me today. There you have it, no answer. I wish she saw me walk across the stage to get my high school diploma, or in the cafeteria at

Tampa Bay Tech to see me sign that Letter of Intent to attend a major University. Maybe it's not as important to her as it is to me. Maybe she likes prison more then she likes being at my life events.
What about the day when I got off the plane in Manhattan Kansas and had to kiss my childhood goodbye. I looked back but she wasn't there to say "I love you, I'm so proud of you. You have truly made me a proud mother." Let's rewind it all the way back. What about that day when I took my first step, and drank out of my first real cup? And my very first day of school. She wasn't there

to kiss me on the forehead and tell me to have a great day. I wasn't able to cry for my mommy because I didn't want her to leave me at daycare alone. Yet I'm here alone because you're still not here after all these years. But I will always love you from a distance until I'm ready to face my fears of looking you into the eyes to ask you these questions.

I know some days may seem weaker than others, but put on your glasses and say, "I am strong and I will accept what God has done for me". Wow, I sound pretty strong right now, but it hasn't been easy guys and

I really want you to know that.

One day I was in the mall getting some new kicks for school and, I kid you not, I looked back and saw my biological mother for the first time in my life. We made awkward eye contact and I knew exactly who she was. I mean I had seen her on the news but this experience was like something that you see in the movies. She came up to me and introduced herself. I really didn't care at the time; all I wanted to do was get some new shoes for my first year of high school. She asked me to take a picture with her and I said yes. She also asked my adopted mom if she could visit me. Then she promised to stay out of jail.

You would never believe who I saw on the news three days later. Yes, I felt miserable and it hurts me to my guts because she broke her promise. I think about that day all the time and imagined the first time we met she would run up to me, pick me up, and say you're so beautiful! I thought I would be able to ask all the questions that I had and she would answer them for me. It didn't turn out that way so at the end of the day I'm still sitting here waiting. I talk to her on the phone every blue moon, but that's not enough. I just really want her to do better for herself and her 10 children out here alone. I want her to be happy and stay out of prison.

Maybe we will never see each other again, but I want her to look up at the sky and know we are looking at the same moon, sun, and stars. When I talk to my mother on the phone she seems very relaxed and comfortable. I don't understand why she doesn't cry her heart out when she hears my voice. Why she doesn't seem excited to talk to me or even ask me how I'm doing. I hope when God gives her a chance to get out, she won't take advantage of it. I hope she tries to meet her two daughters who probably don't know she exists. I wish my mother nothing but the best and I just want her to know that her fifth child loves her no matter what.

I dedicate this chapter to the missing piece of my heart and the lonely nights I cry thinking about my mother. If you don't take anything else from this chapter, please understand that just because my parents haven't been here doesn't mean I'm against them in any way. But I will push myself to be better than them and express my feelings.

THINGS IVE LEARNED FROM MY EXPERIENCE...

1. Look at my situation as a blessing.

2. Stay positive.

3. Try and help others.

Why is everyone laughing at me?

I pretty much got laughed at for everything you could think of. I got laughed at for being tall, I got laughed at for being "lame". I don't party that much and I had never had sex. So, I didn't fit in with the girls my age. I was the scary girl. I was confused on what I wanted and who I wanted.

One moment in time I felt like I was born to be gay because nobody liked me. But then I started growing a little booty and grew up, and the boys came like roaches. I pulled my spray out and ended up killing them all. I wouldn't have sex with any of them so they stopped liking me.

All the people I thought were my friends laughed at me because I was still a virgin. I thought about having sex to fit in, but God came running and said "you better get your life".

Some of you are out there with kids but have no job. Your kid's father is just your baby daddy and not your husband. Let's try to get our priorities in order before we think about having children ladies. Let's earn some respect and stop giving it up so easily. Ask yourself some of these questions before you open your legs.

Did you finish school? I hear a lot of people say, "school isn't for me". Well how do you know? Did you try it? Why do you feel like school isn't for you? I don't understand that statement at all, but one thing you can't do is force someone to do something they don't want to do. Companies are looking for educated folks, someone who can run his or her company.

Do you have a good job where you're making enough money to provide for your child and yourself? It might not be any of my business but where do you work? Burger King? Wal-Mart? Ross? That's a playhouse check and you deserve to be working somewhere

where you're happy and enjoy waking up to go to work every day.

Are you living a comfortable life? You shouldn't have to beg your baby daddy to buy your son/daughter some shoes. You shouldn't have to trick for some cash every month to pay your bills. You're better than that and you deserve much more. Don't let anyone make you feel like your less than a 10.

If you feel like you're doing all the right things keep doing it, but at the end of the day be honest with yourself. I'm not here to judge you or tell you what to do, but make sure you are not getting pressured to do something that you aren't ready for. You should out-think the people that are laughing at you. Laughing gets you unnecessary attention. Be the lame kid that everyone whispers about. Trust me 99.9% of their information will be false. Don't get discouraged. Let them laugh now, they're going to get tired eventually. Stay in class extra time to get more help, wait until you're ready to have sex or even a boyfriend, and if your friends laugh at you for doing the right things then they aren't your friends so you know what to do, leave their a** alone.

Someone's opinion of

you doesn't have to become your reality. You are the company you attract, so be careful. Let them laugh from the other side of the fence, they aren't coming over because they fear a challenge. I still get laughed at for my dreams, but God knows what I want to do and it will happen if I keep working my butt off and keep him first in my life.

I know I talked about a lot in this chapter, but I tried to hit every possible reason a young lady fails. I dedicate this chapter to all the kids that try to be something they aren't. Be the seed, don't rush and try to automatically be the plant. You need sunlight and water first, then one day you'll grow into this amazing plant that shines like no other.

Vision Board...
Insert your goals,
dreams & aspirations.

I want to be a millionaire NOW

If I learn how to sing could I have a life like Beyoncé? If I work on my game could I be where LeBron is and live like him? If I read books on how to be successful in life would that prevent me from hitting a wall?

A lot of us watch inspirational videos on YouTube such as Will Smith, ET, Les Brown, etc. Don't get me wrong, I think that's one of the main processes to success, but realistically that's not enough. Not everyone gets on the internet to watch something positive. Our generation is focused on who liked our picture on Instagram, who tweeted us, who texted someone else's boy.

I'm not a millionaire, but I sure as hell think like one. I'm always trying to find ways to be successful. I watch the people I want to live like and be like, from T.I to Obama. If negative is left, I'm going right.

Sometimes I have a vision that I'm going to the Grammy Awards to watch an amazing show. I imagine that I am out to eat with Obama and Michele. I can't forget to call up my girls Tiny and Toya for brunch in Italy. I'll text Will Smith later to see if he wants to shoot a movie with me. I have to text the

OMG girls to see if they
are doing well.

If you had a chance
to go inside my mind you'd
probably think I'm crazy.
On Monday I might want
to be a fashion designer,
but Tuesday I'm going to
singing lessons. Wednesday
I'm writing a book, but
Thursday I'm on air talking
about the latest fashion of
2014, and Friday I'm having
a book signing. You must
have something that makes
you stand out. You must
own the world and not be
afraid to get knocked down.
When life knocks you down
try laying on your back,
because if you can look up
you can get up.
What is it that will help

you get back up again? Les Brown - I love that man because he's so powerful. Find yourself and make sure you are who you want to be. Change is free, so keep changing until you find the right you.

I dedicate this chapter to imagination and change. Imagine you can be anything you want and know you have the power to change if it doesn't work out for you.

My Family...

Let me start off by saying I love my family. I thank God that I am blessed to have these wonderful people in my life. Everyone has a dysfunctional family, but my family is for real for real dysfunctional. We are far from perfect, not even close. But at the end of the day I wouldn't trade them in for any other. My family is my WHY, and I hope when they look at me they see greatness. I want them to understand that anything is possible.

Everyone in my family knows how to do hair but "ME".

They are extremely

talented. Sometimes I don't think they understand that. My family has it all. We are athletic and creative.

Four years ago, I decided that I didn't want to go to college in Florida. I took a big jump and went all the way to Kansas. People thought I was crazy. As of right now, I don't have any regrets about the choice I made. Throughout this experience, I realized that staying with my family wouldn't have provided me any growth. I would have been comfortable and in the same place forever. I have seen so many people my age get stuck in Tampa, and they had more talent than me. If you don't take that jump right away it's hard to get motivated to do it later. I have seen half of the world and I am just 22 years old.

Life is all about adaptability and survival. I'm writing books, creating websites, designing my own Brand and shooting hoops, because God gave me these talents. I want the younger generation of my family to see me doing positive things and say, "I want to be like Erica, she's amazing." I came from nothing, and I've seen my family struggle here and there. I don't want to be like that. No, I'm not better than anybody, but I will say that I want a better life.

The hood gets old and starts to fade away after a while. My dreams are bigger and I want to be above. I know that I can't sit under my family all day and expect to get better. They are amazing people to visit, but I don't want to go back where I came from anytime soon. I'm moving forward in life and setting examples for them.

As you get older, realize that family can be everything, but you sometimes must separate yourself for a while in order to be successful. Have fun on Christmas and Thanksgiving, b u t understand that you have business to take of after. If they don't understand where you're trying to go, don't talk about it to anyone, just do it. You have a dream, go after it, and the people who love you will still have your best interest. I am proud to say that I am the first out of nine from my biological mother to graduate from high school and to go to college. It's sad that some of my sisters and brothers don't want to do anything, but I really hope this book, and everything else I am, will change their lives. I love to see others doing great too, and why not try and help the people who are closet to my life.

I dedicate this chapter to my dysfunctional family. I love You guys.

*I want you to step outside your comfort zone for one day.

 - Make a list of 5 family members, call them and share something that's on your mind whether its "girl I really want to open a shop" or I was just calling to say I love you."

1. _____

2._____

3._____

4._____

5._____

What time is it?

NEVER SAY THIS. "What time is it?" Why do you want to know what time it? Everyone has 24 hours/ 1,440 minutes/ 86,400 seconds in a day. Have a plan for your life. You need to be too busy every day to think about the time.

Always remember that the person next to you is working even harder than you. If you're doing absolutely nothing with your life don't even think about talking or hating on others. You have just as much time as they do to be successful. What makes you stand out more is actually trying to do something for yourself, even if you make mistakes. I'm not talking about a job at McDonald's, Wal-Mart, or the mall. God has created a talent inside of you so don't be selfish. Use it and find a way to be comfortable with your life. Have fun and enjoy what you do. You literally have one time to live this life so make the rest of your life the best of your life.

I understand that many people have made mistakes in their life and it's hard finding a job, but I'm here to tell you that I'm a tough lover and I DON'T CARE what you went through. That's your past so paint your future now. Get your butt up and be great. Create a job and be your own boss. You do the hiring and help others as well. Time is a very important tool in life and you shouldn't take it for granted. The road will come as you take each step. You don't get in life what you want, you get in life what you are. So be great and create a job. Use the time that is given to you to become successful.

I dedicate this chapter to the remainder amount of time in your life to be great at something you love and enjoy.

Crush

That boy you thought you loved is over there cheating on you right now. He's flirting with the pretty girl that has been passed around to all his homeboys. She has no respect for herself so she is used to being broken down. You just knew that he would be the perfect guy for you. Your friends are trying to tell you what's up, but you don't want to hear it because you're "drunk in love". Half of the crowd is telling you that you two make a cute couple and the other half is saying how stupid you are behind your back because they just saw him with another chick in T building. Ladies, if a man can't respect you, you don't need him.

I met a boy in high school I fell in love with. He broke my heart into pieces. I still have love for this dude, but I will not be disrespected. Deep down in my heart I just knew that we would spend the rest of our lives together. I had his back in everything and supported him like I was supposed to. At the end of the day, my loyalty didn't mean anything to him. I realized God didn't want me to have a man at that time, so I was forced to learn how to love myself.

Love is a beautiful thing and I'm not telling

you to be single for the rest of your life, but please take your time and don't get hurt. Just because he has two legs and two arms doesn't make him right for you. I get lonely a lot, and want someone I can call every night and say, "goodnight baby", but I am patient enough to wait on God to send me the right man.

Dudes, realize that when you let a good woman go she probably won't come back because of the way you have treated her. Another man is already treating her well. Let's be smart about everything. You think it's cool to have "hoes", but how cool will it be to have AIDS? Not funny anymore, huh? And please stop referring to us as "bitches". Last time I checked I was a young African American female. If you can't respect me, get away. Ladies, don't allow a dude to call you other than your name. That's the most disrespectful thing ever.

My first love gave me my first promise ring for Christmas, and inside it read "true   love waits." He was right because I am still waiting for true love. My future love will come around one day and he's going be amazing. Ladies, God is saving us for an amazing handsome young man. I promise you God is going to send you Mr. Right. If you have a boyfriend who respects you, then you go girl and I wish you many happy years. If you're married, congratulations and I wish you nothing but success on those nights when you're fighting. If you're being heart-broken LEAVE him, he's not worth your time. There are too many men in the world to be stressing over one who disrespects you. The man that I will fall in love with and marry is writing a book right now about his life, and we are going to meet up one day. I know God has Mr. Right waiting for me.

In dedicate this chapter to my first love. Thank you for teaching me life lessons, you turned out to be an important factor in my life. God bless your two children. I pray your son treats ladies with respect, and your daughter doesn't get her heart broken by someone like yourself. I was living a damn fairy tale...

Did you have a crush? How was that experience for you? Send me an email!!!
Weareforeveryoung1@gmail.com

Lost loved ones

I don't take death well. And I don't understand it at all. I believe in God, but why do the ones you love go so soon? How do you love someone your whole life and then they can be gone in the blink of an eye? Sometimes you're aware that someone is going to die and you're able to say a few words, but then some people die without a warning. It's all crazy to me.

I have had some amazing people in my life who aren't here today, and I have learned something from each of them. They all taught me a lesson that I will never forget. Kids

lose their mother and
father now-a-days and I
don't have the words to say
to them, but I will say I'm
sorry for your loss. I take
my hat off to you because
you are strong and
continue to be that way.

I have cried many
times because I have lost
someone important in my
life. At one point, I lost
three friends in two
months. I lost my
grandfather at age eight,
and it was very hard
because I was very close
to him. That man had my
back every time I got in
trouble. I just wish he
were here to see all the
great things I am doing. I
lost my God-brother my

last year in AAU basketball and it tore me apart. I lost my uncle in 2016. He was my best friend.

I know it hurts everyone, but I'm here to let you know you can overcome it. Keep praying and remember all the good times you had. Also, don't hate people or treat them bad because their time can end at any point. My God-grandmother lost her husband and it happened so quickly. His birthday was two days before he passed away. They woke up and she went in the living room for a few minutes, came back in the bedroom and he was gone. Love your loved ones. Life has no time limit   for anyone.

I dedicate this chapter to all my lovely angels looking down on me. I know you all are doing great. This chapter is also for your lost loved ones as well. May you be able to live on with less pain.

Ps: Wish heaven had visitation... What would you tell your loved ones if you could speak to them one more time?

_____

_____

_____

_____.

3200

I grew up on the streets and had a lot of friends. You'll take a bullet for your home-girl or home-boy, right? You're down for your hood and no one can disrespect it, huh? Look at your surroundings and ask yourself, do you really want to live like that. If you think it's a great life, then I'm not going to stop you but be smart. You have friends that turn on you, close friends die because they were at the wrong place at the wrong time; have fights with mom and she starts to worry if you would be alive later; and that good old candy lady down the street getting everybody's money.

Guys listen, live your life but don't do it in the streets. If you can't see that the streets are dangerous and deadly, you need to wake up. I've lost some close friends and family members in the streets and it's not fun. Some deaths were a mistake, being somewhere they didn't belong. boys get your money another way. Hmm, let's see, how about you get a job or create a legal job and stay safe.

Ladies, I haven't forgotten about you. Don't lay down with these dudes and think they love you because they really don't. They just need somewhere to lay their head (and get some) for the night. One second they're saying they love you and moments later you have a black eye for liking some dude's picture on Instagram. You don't need that in your life. Find a nice, young, handsome man out there, or wait for God to send you someone.

The streets may seem fun at first, but when someone dies everyone is emotional and ready to find the killer. I've had my moments being at the park as a child and throwing up the gang sign. I still tell people that I'm from 32nd Ellicott. That's not my hang out spot but that's where I was raised. I have pride for my hood and nothing will change that. When I go back home I visit some of my childhood friends and just look up and thank God that I made it. I wish that people in my hood could understand that life has so much to offer. Half of them probably haven't been past Orlando, and that's sad because its only 45 minutes away from Tampa. I am living a great life, but I will never forget where I came from.

Lastly, parents, don't allow your child to run in the streets like they are grown. Take action in their life and be a part of it. Show them the world.

Maybe they think the streets love them more than you do. Maybe they go to the hood because you're always in the club on Friday nights turning up. Instead, maybe go on a movie date with your child, or tell them how much you love them. Help them with their homework from time to time, or go to their after s c h o o l activities.
Wait, I think this one would be great... COOK for them.

I dedicate this chapter to not forgetting where you came from, but understanding that it's okay to grow out of it. <u>I will never forget where I ate frozen cups and boiled peanuts.</u>

Why didn't he
teach me how
to ride a bike?

They tell me you were this outstanding basketball player. You were the man of the town and everyone respected you. Everyone loved game day because you were the show of the night. You seem to have everyone's back but mine. Where were you when I needed to learn how to ride my first bike? Why didn't you teach me the game of basketball? Why wasn't my father here when I needed him? It's bad enough I didn't know who my mother was. I went to camps and saw everyone else's father with them, but where was mine?

Recently I found out

my father gave up his right for me when I was younger. How was that even possible? It wasn't my fault you had me. Why couldn't you take on the responsibility of taking care of me until my mom came back? You raised your stepchildren and had a beautiful family.

Christmas was the saddest for me because all the grandchildren got five or six gifts and I was lucky to get two. I was disappointed to open my gifts and only see a pair of house slippers or a bottle of lotion. I wanted to go to my father's house a lot, but when I went I spent more time with my step-mama than I did with my actual father. He was always too busy for me. As I got older I found myself hating him and not even wanting to go anymore. It was a waste of my time and I felt like I was begging for him to love me.

Have you ever felt like a lost child? Like no one understands what you are going through? The pain inside your heart is like acid. All I ever wanted was to live happily ever after with a big family.

People tell me all the time that we look alike, play alike and act alike, but I have no clue because I don't know you. I'm the lost child. I felt like when my father was trying to be in my life it was to get attention. People are always coming up to me saying your father is always talking great things about you and is so proud of his baby girl. See, now I'm lost because every moment I shined he wasn't there. He has probably come to four of my high school games total. He came to one of my college games. My father came to my high school graduation and did not give me anything. He also came to my graduation party and, once again, I did not get anything from him. I'm not asking for anything, but it really hurts me inside that he doesn't care. Well at least that's how I feel. For 22-years you didn't have to worry about taking care of me, didn't have to spend a dime on me and I can't even get something as simple as love from my own father.

I am going to make sure my child grows up with a father because it's just not fun. Your father is supposed to be your best friend, but I don't think I can trust mine with a piece of my mind. I'm not trying to talk trash about him, I just want him to know how I feel inside.

Since I'll never be able to tell him this in person, never in life, I dedicate this chapter to him.

A lot of you know what's it like growing up without a father. It's tough and I understand what you are going through. Everything is going to be okay. All I can tell you is don't make the mistakes that your parents made. Be better than them and show them how it's supposed to be done. I love the saying "no matter what your father or mother was, you can be better." That's what I have always stuck to, and I believe that saying. When your nights get dark and you're feeling lonely, remember that everything happens for a reason and

God makes no mistakes.
Keep your head up and be
better.

Dear daddy,

_____
_____
_____
_____
_____
_____
_____
_____
_____
_____
_____
_____.

Sincerely, _____

Thank You

You raised me and made me who I am today. I just want to take the time to say thank you for taking me in when I was a baby. Thanks for leading me in all the right directions in life and just being a lifetime supporter in everything I do. You're a rock star and I may not show you all the time that I love and appreciate what you do, but if it weren't for you I probably wouldn't have love for the game or be into fashion.

I am the luckiest girl in the world. I got to see half of the world as a teenager, met some amazing people, got spoiled with everything I wanted and didn't need. This lady showed me things I would have never seen if I was with my biological mother or father. She gave her whole life up so that I could live mine, and baby girl I can't say thank you enough. You made it to every single basketball game and event I had in my life. You were there to see me take my first steps, ride a bike, model, and play sports. You were there to see me get every award I ever earned. You made sure I got the extra help I needed to continue my education. You traveled to every single state with me and helped me make the hardest decision of my life. You were right there to see me sign my Letter of Intent and walk across that stage to receive my high school diploma. You were there to send me off to college and say I'm so proud of everything you are doing. You always made me feel like a 10 even on my worst days. I can't name one thing you weren't at. You made sure I had somewhere to sleep and something to eat every night for 18 years.

You are one amazing women and I feel sorry for the people who never got a chance to see that part of you. You were very annoying at times but it was all worth it. You made me realize I don't need a man to make me happy, and that no dream is too big. Such a good-hearted woman with so much love in your heart. Thank you for everything you have done in my life. Thanks for taking my mother and father's responsibility and making it your own. I really appreciate everything you do.

Why not dedicate this chapter to my wonderful adopted mother "Cheryl Young"! Thank for molding me into a smart, well-mannered young lady. You're the real MVP and I love you.

Relationships

Either I have really bad luck or I pick the worst dudes to talk to. I know what I want, but settling isn't in the equation. My childhood has everything to do with the men I chose.

When I was little, I spent the night at this lady's house who had taken me and her children to the fair. I slept on the couch and when I woke up my panties were sitting on top of me. I couldn't believe what was happening. Someone had touched me inappropriately while I was asleep. I kept this inside for many years, and then one day I went to an event and the speaker asked us to raise our hands if we had been rapped before. As soon as I lifted my hand, everyone looked at me in total shock. I still remember the feeling of his cold hands in my pants rubbing his fingers on my clit. What hurts the most was not being able to trust anyone. I was clearly taken advantage of as a little girl.

The first boy I ever talked to has four kids now. God really saved me from that. We texted and talked on the phone 24/7, but he didn't want the title of being in a relationship. I also found out he was dating my friend. I watched him bring her a

Valentine gift in the gym of Memorial Middle School. That was all the dudes I talked to. Nobody wanted to go past friendship. I wanted so much more.

Then I met this dude my first year in high school. He was a senior. Again, we talked all the time but he was just trying to have a "friend with benefits". I remember he texted me one day and asked if he could be my first. I had no idea what he was taking about so I asked someone. They said that he wanted to be the first to have sex with me. I told him yes, but we all know the story didn't end like that. He graduated and

I got over him. He's in a relationship now with a beautiful baby girl.

When I transferred schools in the 9th grade I met my high school love, well at least I thought he was. I was the new kid on the block so I was an easy target. I also was known as the girl that came to Tech to play ball. Then I was introduced to the dude I talked about in the "crush chapter." FINALLY, I was in a relationship. I didn't know that it would come with pain, hurt, and lies. I broke up with him before I went to college. Although he didn't take my virginity, I felt like he took my heart and ran it over five times. I hated him for cheating on me and then going off to college, also for not finishing school and ball, going from girl to girl, and having two children.

My college sophomore year, I lost my virginity to someone who wasn't even worth it. We had been talking for about three months. He was so cocky and completely stopped taking to me after we had sex.

I used to mess with another dude, who later I found out was in a relationship. I wanted so much in my life at that time, so I had to end it even though I didn't want to.

I will not go into details about my second relationship, but after lowering my standards for this boy in so many ways, I got cheated on so bad. This young man was in a relationship for five years with a girl back home. She wrote me on social media in a respectful way. I was so embarrassed I ended it and started talking to this other dude.

Now this dude was younger but he respected me, kissed me on my forehead, told me he loved me, checked on me, etc. He was so perfect, but he didn't want to be in a relationship and I did. We are friends now, but I was so sad because I felt like I had found exactly what I was looking for in a man, but it was too good to be true.

There you have it ladies and gentlemen. A pretty face means nothing. I have such bad luck when it comes to men.

I want to dedicate this chapter to all the men I've mentioned. You all taught me something really important, to love myself first. I wish you guys the very best in your lives and thanks so much for the lessons.

Dear New York...

In Neeeewww
Yooorrrrkkkk!!!!

Anyone who knows me knows that I am obsessed with New York City. I have always told people that I am from there. There's something about the city that makes a girl believe she can become whatever she wants. My dream job is to be a part of the BET family one day. I want my book to become a New York Best Seller as well. I just wanted to quickly shout out my ego's hometown. Imagine you can become anything, go anywhere, and be whatever you want.

This mini chapter is dedicated to my future home.

Lasts Few Words

I want to share some things with you before you close this book. First, let me take the time to say thanks for reading my book. I hope I inspired someone with at least one chapter. This book is designed to help you while sharing my story. I had to let go of some things to grow. At the end of each chapter I dedicated it to something or someone. I think it's important for us to talk about our problems, but then appreciate and accept what has happened in our lives.

I want to share something really important with you all before I go. I started writing this book in

May of 2013, and made a promise to myself that I would have it ready before I graduated from college. GOAL ACCOMPLISHED... But I want to thank God for allowing me to finish. I almost didn't finish this book. Not because I was lazy or anything, but because I tried to kill myself in 2014 and 2016.

I almost over dosed and lost my life. The doctor told me if I would have taken one more pill I would have died in my sleep. I had never been so scared in my life. I had a block in front of me and I felt like I couldn't move anywhere. I lost so much that year from family, friends, basketball, etc. I was just tired of everything and everyone. I wanted everyone who hurt me to feel the pain I was feeling. I got fed up with being the person always there for everyone, but no one was there for me.

I survived my suicide attempt. I'm happy to be alive and sharing with all you wonderful people. I'm so blessed and I want to congratulate you on finishing this book and graduating with me. WE DID IT BABY!!! 2017 What'sss poppinnnnn Yo!

I _____

Sign this contract to show that
I will not settle in life ever
again. I am better than
what they think I am. I
understand that in order for
me to succeed in life I have
to accept the fact that
everyone CAN'T come.

Made in the USA
Lexington, KY
09 July 2018